Happy Parents Raise Happy Children

A Joyful Home is the Best Classroom

By

SANAH S

★ ★ ★ ★

WHY IS THIS BOOK FOR YOU?

Parenting is one of the most profound and rewarding responsibilities in life. This book is designed to guide you toward positive parenting, offering insights and strategies to help you nurture a strong, healthy, and meaningful relationship with your child.

A child's development is shaped more by parental influence than by the school they attend. A secure, loving bond with parents fosters confidence, emotional well-being, and positive social interactions.

In today's fast-paced world, building and maintaining this ideal relationship can be challenging, but with the right approach, it is achievable.

This book provides practical strategies to help you raise happy, confident, and successful children. While parenting styles may differ, the foundation of a child's happiness and success ultimately rests on the relationship they share with their parents.

A happy couple creates a happy home, and a happy home nurtures a happy child.

When a child is born, they are like a blank canvas—full of potential, waiting to be shaped by love, guidance, and care. So, dear reader, pick up your brush and paint your masterpiece.

Acknowledgments

This book would not have been possible without the love, guidance, and unwavering support of so many incredible people in my life. My deepest gratitude goes to:

✦ The Creator of this Universe – for blessing me with the opportunity to touch lives, inspire change, and make a meaningful difference.

✦ My Parents – My first teachers, who not only gave me life but also shaped my values with wisdom, love, and resilience. "Thank you" is far too small a word for the endless sacrifices you both have made for me—I love you beyond words.

✦ My Life Partner – My rock, my strength, and my greatest supporter. Your unwavering belief in me has been my anchor in every storm.

✦ My Elder Sister – The one who has stood beside me since the very first day of my life. You are my confidante, my guide, and my forever source of strength. I love you endlessly.

✦ My Younger Brother – With quiet strength and unwavering love, you have always been there. Thank you for the silent support, the loud laughter, and the countless cherished memories—I love you.

✦ My Childhood, School, and College Friends – Each one of you holds a special place in my heart. Your love, support, and companionship have been the greatest blessings in my life's journey. I am forever grateful.

✦ Heartfelt gratitude to my grandmother in heaven, who played the most vital role in my education and upbringing. She once told me, ***"Your fingers are meant to hold a pen, not a scrubber."*** Today, she would be happy and proud. Grandmother, I have held onto the pen, just as you wished. "Lots of love" and "thank you" feel like small words compared to what you mean to me.

✦ Thank you to every Guru who has taught me. I am who I am because of each of you. Heartfelt gratitude to all my Gurus, from kindergarten to school, to college, and even today.

This book is a tribute to all of you—your love, your encouragement, and the light you bring into my life. Thank you from the depths of my heart.

Introduction

Welcome to Parenting is an Art: A Guide to Positive Parenting for a Healthy and Happy Child—a journey that will help you explore the profound role of parents in shaping their children's lives while embracing the artistry of parenting.

Every parent is an artist, and this guide equips you with the knowledge and tools to craft your greatest masterpiece: a happy, resilient, and well-rounded child. More than that, it helps you foster a lasting, enriching relationship with your child, built on understanding and love.

Table Of Contents

CHAPTER 1: THE ESSENCE OF PARENTHOOD: A TIMELESS RESPONSIBILITY

Parenting is an intrinsic part of society, a journey that transcends species and highlights the fundamental need for guidance, especially in a child's formative years. While parenting has evolved over centuries, it remains one of life's most vital responsibilities, shaping the future of humanity.

Mastering this pivotal skill is not merely an option; it is essential. As a parent, you become an architect of tomorrow, nurturing and shaping the next generation. It is both a great responsibility and a cherished privilege, as you hold the key to moulding the future of the human race.

Congratulations on undertaking this extraordinary milestone. In the upcoming chapters, we are set to embark on a journey together, sharing easily accessible and implementable life hacks.

These insights are crafted to guide you through every stage of your child's development, empowering you to be the unparalleled parent your child could ever envision.

Together, let's navigate the intricacies of parenthood and unlock the potential to create a nurturing and fulfilling environment for your growing family.

Understanding Parenthood: A Definition

"The process of raising and nurturing children, encompassing various responsibilities such as providing emotional and physical support, guidance, education, and instilling values."

Parenting is the process of raising and nurturing children. This involves taking care of children as they grow up, providing the things they need and helping them develop.

Parenthood is a profound and universal human experience that transcends geographical, cultural, and historical boundaries. Regardless of where one stands on the globe or which era one finds themselves in, the journey of parenting is a shared narrative that echoes through time. At its core, parenthood speaks to a fundamental aspect of human existence, linking generations and weaving a tapestry of interconnected lives.

From ancient civilizations to contemporary societies, the universal nature of parenthood lies in its essence—the commitment to nurturing and guiding the next generation. While specific practices and cultural norms may vary, the inherent desire to protect, love, and shape the lives of the young remains a constant. Whether in the heart of a bustling metropolis or a remote village, the emotional currents of parenthood are remarkably similar. The joys of a child's first steps, the challenges of sleepless nights, and the profound responsibility of molding a young mind are threads that weave through the collective human experience.

Across cultures, the universal language of parental love is spoken through gestures, expressions, and sacrifices. It is witnessed in the tender lullabies sung to soothe a crying infant, the patient teaching of life skills, and the unwavering support provided during times of adversity. Parenthood, in its universal form, unites individuals under the banner of shared responsibility for the well-being and development of the next generation.

The commonality of the parenting experience extends beyond cultural idiosyncrasies to encompass the intrinsic human need for connection and belonging. Parenthood is a bridge that connects individuals to their roots, as traditions are passed down from one generation to the next. It is a beacon that guides families through the ebb and flow of life, fostering a sense of continuity and stability.

Encompassing Various Responsibilities:

- **Providing Emotional and Physical Support:**

Parents comfort their children when they're sad or scared (emotional support), and they also make sure their children have things like food, a home, and clothes (physical support).

- **Guidance:**

Parents give advice and help their children make good choices. For example, a parent might guide their child on how to solve a problem or make a decision.

- **Education:**

Parents play a big role in helping their children learn. This includes teaching them things at home and being involved in their school life.

- **Instilling Values:**

Parents teach their children about what is right and wrong, and they help them develop good qualities. For instance, a parent might teach a child the importance of honesty or kindness.

In simple terms, parenting is like being a guide and supporter for your children, making sure they have what they need, helping them learn, and teaching them how to be good people.

Your core values and beliefs are deeply rooted in our upbringing, shaped by the principles instilled in us during childhood. Let's explore how sacred texts have imparted timeless wisdom on parenting.

Bible (Christianity):

"Train up a child in the way he should go; even when he is old, he will not depart from it." - Proverbs 22:6

Quran (Islam):

"And those who say, 'Our Lord, grant us from among our wives and offspring comfort to our eyes and make us an example for the righteous.'" - Quran 25:74

Bhagavad Gita (Hinduism):

"The soul is born into delusion, for the protection of the good, the destruction of the wicked, and the establishment of righteousness, I am born in every age." - Bhagavad Gita 4:7-8

Tripitaka (Buddhism):

"The child has duties towards the parents. Thus, should he look after them who, having brought him up, brought him into the world and reared him, just as I, having begotten him, brought him up and reared him." - Sigalovada Sutta

Guru Granth Sahib (Sikhism):

"One who loves the Lord, and understands the dynamics of spiritual wisdom, has the perfect understanding of the Way of Life. His family, which once suffered in separation, joins together and finds peace." - Guru Granth Sahib, 524

Torah (Judaism):

"Honor your father and your mother, that your days may be long in the land that the Lord your God is giving you." - Exodus 20:12

Dhammapada (Buddhism):

"If by renouncing a lesser happiness, one may realize a greater happiness, let the wise person renounce the lesser, having regard for the greater." - Dhammapada 290

In the next chapter, we will explore the various parenting styles and their impact on both children and parents. By the end, you will have a deeper understanding of your own parenting approach and how it shapes your relationship with your child.

CHAPTER 2: CONSCIOUS PARENTING: NURTURING YOURSELF AND YOUR RELATIONSHIPS

As a parenting coach, I emphasize the transformative power of self-awareness and conscious parenting. This chapter delves into the profound responsibility of raising children and the imperative need for parents to embark on their journey of self-discovery before guiding their offspring.

I was truly awestruck while listening to Sadhguru on YouTube one day, where he shared a profound insight: "Raise yourself before you raise your kids." This simple yet powerful statement highlights the essence of conscious parenting.

Sadhguru teaches that parenting isn't about controlling or molding a child into our expectations but about creating an environment of love, understanding, and growth. To do this, we must first address our own emotional baggage, unresolved issues, and personal limitations.

Our children learn far more from observing our actions, attitudes, and behaviours than from our words. By elevating our awareness and becoming our best version, we naturally create a nurturing space where our children can thrive.

Self-awareness is a crucial aspect of effective parenting, as it lays the foundation for building healthy and meaningful connections with our children. Understanding oneself—emotions, triggers, and personal values—profoundly influences the way we navigate the complex terrain of parenthood.

When parents cultivate self-awareness, they gain insights into their own strengths and limitations, fostering a more empathetic and responsive approach to their child's needs.

In the realm of parenting, self-awareness allows individuals to recognize and regulate their emotional responses, providing a stable and secure environment for children. Acknowledging one's emotions without judgment enables parents to model emotional intelligence, teaching children valuable lessons in empathy and self-expression.

Additionally, self-awareness empowers parents to break the cycle of reactive behaviours, fostering a more thoughtful and intentional parenting style.

Furthermore, self-awareness is instrumental in shaping parenting values and beliefs. As parents become attuned to their core principles, they can make intentional choices that align with their values, creating a consistent and nurturing environment for their children.

This self-reflection also facilitates open communication with children about family values, establishing a foundation for shared understanding and mutual respect.

In times of challenge or conflict, self-aware parents can pause and assess their reactions, making room for thoughtful responses rather than impulsive reactions. This not only reduces tension within the parent-child relationship but also demonstrates the importance of mindfulness and self-regulation to children.

The ability to communicate effectively with children relies on a deep understanding of one's own communication style, allowing parents to adapt and tailor their approach to the unique needs of each child.

Here are some common beliefs and conditioning patterns we may have absorbed subconsciously. Let's take a closer look at a few of them and explore their impact.

Children are a Gift, Not Possessions:

The fundamental perspective to embrace is that children are not possessions or future investments. Rather, they are unique beings, a gift that comes through parents but does not belong to them. Treating children as property or future assets is a grave injustice to the creation and the Creator, inviting a hefty price in the form of distorted lives and missed opportunities.

Example:

Consider the case of parents who view their children as an extension of themselves, moulding their lives to fulfill their unfulfilled dreams or societal expectations. This approach stifles the child's individuality and hinders the blossoming of their true potential.

Liberating Your Children:

Parents must liberate their children from the shackles of predetermined expectations. Before having children, thoughtful consideration is essential, and for those already on the parenting journey, a serious reflection is necessary. The aspiration should be to nurture a generation that surpasses the current one.

Example:

Imagine a parent who, instead of imposing their unfulfilled ambitions on their child, creates an environment that encourages the child to explore and discover their unique talents and passions.

Transitioning from Boss to Friend:

During the formative years until around the age of 12, children may be more receptive to parental guidance. However, after this phase, they crave companionship rather than a boss within the household. The shift from a commanding presence to a friendly guide is crucial for fostering healthy parent-child dynamics.

Example:

Reflect on your own experiences growing up – did you appreciate being talked down to or dictated to? Children, too, seek understanding, empathy, and a friend who can guide them through the intricacies of life.

Respecting Your Child's Intelligence:

Parents must question their assumption of being inherently more intelligent than their children. While external influences may pose challenges, fostering an environment that empowers children to think for themselves is critical.

Example:

Encourage open dialogue with your child, allowing them to express their thoughts and opinions without fear of retribution. This approach builds trust and nurtures their innate intelligence.

Protecting Without Imposing Fear:

Parents should strive to protect their children from negative influences while simultaneously instilling the courage to make informed decisions independently.

Example:

Rather than instilling fear in the child, create an atmosphere where they feel confident in seeking guidance when needed. This approach helps them develop critical thinking skills and the ability to make informed choices.

Observation and Questioning:

Children possess a keen sense of observation, often manifesting in a cascade of questions. Parents should embrace this curiosity and answer their queries honestly, acknowledging when they don't know the answer.

Example:

A parent who encourages their child's questioning nature and admits to not having all the answers sets the foundation for honest communication and fosters a sense of curiosity and learning.

Handling Privilege Responsibly:

Parents must respect the privilege of being entrusted with the upbringing of a child. Cherishing this privilege involves creating an atmosphere conducive to the child's growth and fostering an environment that aligns with the values parents wish to instill.

Example:

Consider a family where parents use their privilege responsibly by creating a loving, open, and nurturing environment that allows the child to observe positive behaviours.

Reflecting to Raise:

In essence, parents should understand that the process of raising children is intricately tied to their own growth. By investing time and effort into becoming better human beings, parents naturally reflect those positive changes onto their children.

Example:

Imagine a parent who, through their actions and behaviours, inspires their child to emulate qualities such as kindness, integrity, and resilience.

The journey of parenting is not merely about guiding children but, fundamentally, about raising oneself. By becoming a beacon of positive change, parents inherently contribute to the creation of a nurturing environment for their children.

As a parenting expert, my advice is clear – raise yourself before you raise your kids, for in doing so, you illuminate the path for the next generation to thrive and blossom.

Reflective Exercise: Nurturing Conscious Parenting

As you embark on the journey of conscious parenting, consider the following exercises to implement the teachings from the earlier chapter:

Self-Reflection:

Take a few moments each day to reflect on your own upbringing. Identify aspects you appreciated in your parents' approach and those you wish were different. Use this reflection to guide your own parenting style.

Positive Affirmations:

Create a list of positive affirmations and consciously integrate them into your daily conversations with your children. Use words that empower, inspire, and nurture their self-esteem.

Quality Time with Kids:

Plan a special outing or activity with your children that promotes bonding and open communication. Engage in activities that allow them to express themselves freely.

Encourage Curiosity:

Foster a culture of curiosity by actively encouraging your children to ask questions. Create an open space where they feel comfortable seeking knowledge and exploring new ideas.

Shift from Boss to Friend:

Reflect on your interactions with your children. Are you primarily acting as a boss, or are you cultivating a friendship? Find moments to share experiences, thoughts, and feelings as equals.

Respect Their Intelligence:

Challenge assumptions of inherent superiority. Engage in conversations where your child's opinions are valued and respected. Embrace the opportunity to learn from each other.

Open Dialogue on Influences:

Initiate a conversation about influences your children may encounter. Discuss how they can navigate external pressures while maintaining their individuality. Encourage them to share their thoughts and concerns.

Balancing Protection and Independence:

Assess how you strike a balance between protecting your children and allowing them independence. Create an environment where they feel safe to make decisions while knowing they can seek guidance when needed.

Observation and Questioning:

Pay attention to your children's observations and questions. Engage in meaningful conversations that not only provide answers but also stimulate their curiosity and love for learning.

Cherish the Privilege:

Remind yourself daily of the privilege it is to be a parent. Create an atmosphere of love, respect, and growth. Cherish the moments you spend together, knowing you are shaping the future through your actions.

Remember, conscious parenting is an ongoing journey of self-discovery and growth. Embrace these exercises with an open heart and a commitment to nurturing a relationship that fosters the well-being and development of both you and your children.

Congratulations on reaching this pivotal milestone in your parenting journey! I invite you to take a moment to reflect and write down three to five actions or practices you will embrace to become a more conscious parent.

1.

____

____

____

2.

____

____

____

3.

____

____

____

4.

____

____

____

5.

____

____

____

The Impact of Parenting on a Child's Future

As parents, we are profoundly responsible for shaping the lives of the little souls entrusted to us. The choices we make in our approach to parenting can significantly influence the paths our children traverse in their future. This chapter delves into the question that often lingers in the minds of parents: Why do some children grow up to engage in destructive behaviours such as theft, substance abuse, fraud, or domestic violence?

The Heavy Cost of Lackluster Parenting:

The emotional toll of inadequate parenting is immeasurable. A child's journey can take unexpected turns if they lack the foundation of a good parenting module. The repercussions extend beyond the individual child to impact society at large.

Protecting Children from Harm:

A parent's approach plays a pivotal role in shielding children from harm. A strong and nurturing bond between parents and children serves as a bulwark against negative behaviour. A secure emotional connection significantly reduces the likelihood of children resorting to destructive paths.

The Vulnerability of Unattended Childhood:

Children left vulnerable without proper parental care often grapple with emotional disorders and low self-esteem. This vulnerability can manifest in various ways, including aggression, depression, the adoption of harmful habits, or even running away from home.

The Lifelong Impact of Neglected Love:

When a child is deprived of love and care, they may struggle to comprehend these fundamental emotions. The absence of such crucial elements can cast a long-lasting shadow on a child's psyche, echoing through their entire life.

The Cycle of Emotional Abuse:

A parent's bad day at work or the severe blow of job loss can inadvertently lead to emotional abuse at home. Yelling, hitting, or speaking harshly to children inflicts emotional wounds that may last a lifetime. Verbal abuse has the potential to sow deep-seated psychological issues that persist into adulthood.

Physical Punishment and its Consequences:

Physical punishment, such as hitting or causing physical pain, can result in severe consequences for a child's mental health. It often contributes to aggressive and negative behaviour patterns that persist into adulthood.

A Bold Message:

In bold letters, let this be a resounding message: Don't bring a child into this world merely to add to the population. Parenthood is a sacred responsibility that should only be undertaken when one is mentally, emotionally, and spiritually prepared to welcome a soul into their life.

Exercise for Reflection:

Reflect on the elements you can incorporate into your child's daily life to foster their well-being.

Consider the changes you can make within yourself to create a happy family and a fulfilling life.

Remember, the journey of parenting is an ongoing commitment to nurturing and guiding our children, and it begins with introspection and a conscious effort to provide the love and care they need to flourish.

CHAPTER 3: THE POWER OF EXAMPLE: HOW YOUR ACTIONS SHAPE YOUR CHILD

In this chapter, we delve into the profound influence that witnessing parental conflicts, neighbourhood disputes, and family struggles can have on children. These experiences not only shape their view of the world but also leave a lasting imprint on their emotional development and future behaviour. Through examining these pivotal moments, we gain insight into how early exposure to such challenges can impact a child's growth and sense of self.

Subconscious Learning and Generational Influence:

Children, even as adults, absorb the environment around them subconsciously. The cells of their bodies bear witness to the harsh realities of the world, illuminated by generations of exposure.

Unfortunately, this has led to instances of domestic abuse persisting through time. As parents, it becomes our responsibility to break this cycle for the betterment of future generations.

Children as Observant Learners:

From the moment a child is born, they begin to learn, both consciously and subconsciously. Witnessing intense instances of abuse or violence can have a direct or indirect impact on a child's mental health, leading to emotional scars, a sense of scarcity, and heightened insecurity.

Real-Life Example:

In my role as a principal, I encountered a heartbreaking incident where a three-year-old child, having witnessed domestic turmoil at home, arrived at school emotionally distressed. The child's plea for help, expressing concern for the well-being of the mother, highlighted the depth of the impact on such young minds. This experience underscored the urgency for intervention and awareness.

Parenting Seminars for Change:

Recognizing the need for change, our school conducted seminars on parenting every quarter to spread awareness and foster healthy parent-child relationships. These sessions proved immensely beneficial, providing both parents and children with valuable insights essential for a happy life.

The Ripple Effect: Impact on Students:

An alarming example was the case of a student who turned to alcohol as a coping mechanism after witnessing his parents' divorce. This heartbreaking outcome emphasizes the importance of handling separation with sensitivity, shielding children from the brutal aspects of the story.

Teaching Resilience and Acceptance:

Another critical aspect highlighted in this chapter is the significance of teaching children to embrace failure. In a world where academic pressures can lead to severe consequences, it is crucial to support children and help them bounce back from setbacks. This involves instilling a resilient mindset and encouraging them to view challenges as opportunities for growth.

Say No to Turbulent Parenting

In our journey as parents, it's easy to become overwhelmed by the challenges and pressures we face daily. Stress, frustration, and fatigue can sometimes lead to moments where our behaviour toward our children becomes less than ideal. However, it is essential to recognize and reject the pattern of turbulent parenting—a style characterized by constant yelling, insulting, and other toxic behaviours.

Turbulent parenting often happens unintentionally. We might lose our temper, raise our voices, or say things in the heat of the moment that we don't truly mean. But these behaviours create lasting emotional scars.

Children subjected to this kind of environment can develop feelings of resentment and hatred, distancing them from their parents. The trust and bond essential for a healthy parent-child relationship erode, leaving behind a legacy of hurt and misunderstanding.

The Lasting Impact of Hurtful Words and Actions

Words and actions, once spoken or taken, cannot be undone. The emotional imprints they leave on a child's mind are enduring. A child's self-esteem, sense of security, and emotional well-being can be profoundly affected by a parent's harsh words or actions.

The negative effects can manifest in various ways, including behavioural issues, academic struggles, and difficulties in forming healthy relationships later in life.

A Clear Message: Avoid Hurtful Behaviours

The message here is clear and urgent: avoid the use of hurtful words or actions. As parents, we must strive to create a nurturing, supportive, and loving environment for our children. This doesn't mean we won't face moments of frustration or anger, but it does mean we must find healthier ways to manage and express these emotions.

Strategies for Healthier Parenting

1. **Pause Before Reacting**: Take a moment to breathe and collect your thoughts before responding to your child. This pause can prevent impulsive reactions that you might later regret.

2. **Communicate Calmly**: Use a calm and steady tone when speaking to your child, even when addressing misbehaviour or issues. This helps maintain a respectful and constructive dialogue.

3. **Set Clear Boundaries and Expectations**: Clearly communicate your expectations and the consequences of not meeting them. Consistent and fair discipline helps children understand boundaries without resorting to yelling or insults.

4. **Seek Support**: If you find it challenging to manage your emotions, seek support from a therapist,

counselor, or parenting group. Professional guidance can provide you with strategies to handle stress and improve your parenting skills.

5. **Model Positive Behaviour**: Children learn by observing their parents. Demonstrating patience, empathy, and respectful communication sets a positive example for them to follow.

Exciting Exercise: Sentences to Avoid versus Sentences to Exchange

The words we choose can either uplift and encourage or inadvertently cause harm. This exercise focuses on identifying sentences to avoid and offering positive alternatives, helping you foster a nurturing and supportive environment.

Avoid: "You always fail at everything."

Encourage: "Everyone faces challenges. Let's figure out how we can learn from this experience."

Avoid: "You're such a disappointment."

Encourage: "I believe in your potential, and I know you can overcome this setback."

Avoid: "You never listen to anything I say."

Encourage: "I appreciate when we can have open and respectful communication."

Avoid: "You're so useless."

Encourage: " Your efforts matter, and I'm here to help you discover your strengths."

Avoid: "You'll never amount to anything."

Encourage: "You have unique talents, and I'm excited to see how you'll shine in your way."

Now that we are aware of the harmful phrases to avoid and the encouraging alternatives to use. Let's take a moment to consider your communication habits, particularly phrases that may have a negative impact. Reflect on these ten common negative statements and propose new, positive alternatives.

This exercise aims to enhance your communication skills and foster more constructive interactions.

Dialogue 1:

Current Negative Statement:

____

____

____

New Positive Statement:

____

____

____

Dialogue 2:

Current Negative Statement:

____

____

____

New Positive Statement:

____

____

____

Dialogue 3:

Current Negative Statement:

____

____

____

New Positive Statement:

____

____

____

Dialogue 4:

Current Negative Statement:

____

____

____

New Positive Statement:

____

____

____

Dialogue 5:

Current Negative Statement:

____

____

____

New Positive Statement:

____

____

____

Dialogue 6:

Current Negative Statement:

____

____

____

New Positive Statement:

____

____

____

Dialogue 7:

Current Negative Statement:

____

____

____

New Positive Statement:

____

____

____

Dialogue 8:

Current Negative Statement:

____

____

____

New Positive Statement:

____

____

____

Dialogue 9:

Current Negative Statement:

____

____

____

New Positive Statement:

____

____

____

Dialogue 10:

Current Negative Statement:

____

____

____

New Positive Statement:

____

____

____

Congratulations! What an incredible journey! I am immensely proud of your wholehearted participation in this exercise. I am confident that your bond with your child will not only strengthen but also flourish. Let's get into more powerful techniques in the next chapter.

CHAPTER 4: NAVIGATING PARENTING STYLES: A COMPASS FOR EFFECTIVE PARENTING

As parents, we embark on a journey that involves not only nurturing our children but also navigating the diverse terrain of parenting styles.

Diana Baumrind, a renowned clinical and developmental psychologist, is widely recognized for her groundbreaking research on parenting styles. In this chapter, I aim to present key insights from her work in my own words, offering a fresh perspective on her influential teachings.

Understanding and recognizing these styles can profoundly impact our approach, influencing the dynamics within our family. In this chapter, we will explore different parenting styles, each contributing its unique flavour to the intricate tapestry of raising children.

Authoritative Parenting: Striking the Balance

Overview: Authoritative parenting is often hailed as a balanced and effective approach. It combines warmth and responsiveness with clear expectations and boundaries. Parents adopting this style engage in open communication with their children, fostering independence while maintaining a nurturing environment.

Key Characteristics:

Communication: Open and two-way communication is encouraged, allowing children to express themselves.

Discipline: Clear rules are set, with consequences explained. Discipline is viewed as a tool for learning rather than punishment.

Warmth: Authoritative parents are warm and supportive, creating a secure emotional foundation.

Example: Sarah, an authoritative parent, sets expectations for her teenager's curfew but engages in a conversation to understand the reasons behind any disagreements, fostering a sense of responsibility.

Authoritarian Parenting: Structure and Rules

Overview: Authoritarian parenting emphasizes structure and adherence to rules. Parents adopting this style often have high expectations and enforce obedience. While structure is crucial, finding a balance with warmth is key.

Key Characteristics:

Rules: Clear and non-negotiable rules are established, with little room for flexibility.

Expectations: High expectations are set, and obedience is valued.

Discipline: Punishments are common for rule violations, with an emphasis on obedience.

Example: James, an authoritarian parent, expects his children to follow a strict schedule for homework and chores, enforcing consequences for any deviation.

Permissive Parenting: The Art of Freedom

Overview: Permissive parenting is characterized by a high degree of warmth and a lenient approach to discipline. While this style fosters a warm and nurturing environment, it can sometimes lack the necessary structure for optimal child development.

Key Characteristics:

Warmth: Permissive parents are nurturing and accepting, often acting as friends to their children.

Discipline: Rules are flexible, and consequences may be inconsistent.

Autonomy: Children are encouraged to explore and make decisions independently.

Example: Emily, a permissive parent, allows her children considerable freedom in choosing their activities and making decisions, sometimes overlooking the need for clear boundaries.

Uninvolved Parenting: Finding a Balance

Overview: Uninvolved parenting is characterized by a lack of emotional involvement and limited responsiveness. While parents in this category may provide for basic needs, emotional support and guidance are often lacking.

Key Characteristics:

Involvement: Limited emotional involvement and responsiveness to a child's needs.

Communication: Communication may be minimal, with little guidance provided.

Independence: Children may develop self-reliance but may lack emotional support.

Example: Mark, an uninvolved parent, provides for his children's basic needs but is often emotionally distant, leaving them to navigate challenges without much guidance.

Blending Styles: The Art of Flexibility

Overview: Many parents find that blending elements of different styles is the key to effective parenting. Flexibility allows parents to adapt to the unique needs of each child, creating a dynamic and responsive approach.

Key Characteristics:

Adaptability: Parents are open to adjusting their approach based on the child's temperament and needs.

Balance: A balanced combination of warmth, structure, and autonomy is maintained.

Communication: Open and ongoing communication fosters a strong parent-child relationship.

Example: Maria, a parent who blends styles, recognizes the importance of setting clear expectations while allowing her children some autonomy. She adjusts her approach based on each child's unique personality.

1. **Parenting Style Quiz**

I have provided two quizzes here to help deepen your understanding of this topic.

Answer the following questions to gain insights into your parenting style. Choose the response that best represents your typical approach in various situations. Keep track of the number of points corresponding to your selected answers to identify your predominant parenting style at the end.

1. When it comes to setting rules for your child:

a) I establish clear and non-negotiable rules (Authoritarian - 3 points)

b) I set rules but am open to discussion and negotiation (Authoritative - 2 points)

c) I have few rules, and flexibility is key (Permissive - 1 point)

d) Rules? I prefer a hands-off approach (Uninvolved - 0 points)

2. How do you handle discipline?

a) I enforce strict consequences for rule violations (Authoritarian - 3 points)

b) I provide consequences but explain the reasons behind them (Authoritative - 2 points)

c) I'm lenient with consequences, focusing on nurturing (Permissive - 1 point)

d) Discipline is not a top priority for me (Uninvolved - 0 points

3. In terms of warmth and emotional support:

a) I believe in showing tough love and emphasizing obedience (Authoritarian - 1 point)

b) I balance warmth with clear expectations (Authoritative - 2 points)

c) I prioritize warmth and acceptance (Permissive - 3 points)

d) Emotional support is not a major focus for me (Uninvolved - 0 points)

4. When your child makes a mistake, your immediate response is to:

a) Apply strict consequences to ensure they learn (Authoritarian - 3 points)

b) Discuss the mistake, explain its impact, and guide them toward a solution (Authoritative - 2 points)

c) Be understanding and forgiving, focusing on learning rather than punishment (Permissive - 1 point)

d) Not intervene; let them handle it independently (Uninvolved - 0 points)

5. How do you approach communication with your child?

a) Communication is primarily directive, emphasizing obedience (Authoritarian - 1 point)

b) I encourage open communication but maintain clear expectations (Authoritative - 2 points)

c) I foster open dialogue, even if it challenges existing rules (Permissive - 3 points)

d) Communication is not a priority for me (Uninvolved - 0 points)

Scoring:

10-12 points: Authoritarian Parenting Style

7-9 points: Authoritative Parenting Style

4-6 points: Permissive Parenting Style

0-3 points: Uninvolved Parenting Style

Take note of your score and refer to the descriptions in the earlier chapter to gain insights into your predominant parenting style. Remember, most parents exhibit a blend of styles, and the quiz is a tool to help you identify your primary approach.

2. Parenting Style Quiz

Choose the answer that best describes how you typically handle situations with your child.

1. How do you set rules for your child?

a) I have clear and non-negotiable rules (Authoritarian)

b) I set rules but am open to discussing them (Authoritative)

c) I have a few rules, but I'm flexible (Permissive)

e) I don't set many rules (Uninvolved)

1. What's your approach to discipline?

a) I enforce strict consequences for breaking rules (Authoritarian)

b) I provide consequences but explain why (Authoritative)

c) I'm lenient with consequences (Permissive)

f) Discipline is not a big concern for me (Uninvolved)

1. How do you show warmth and emotional support?

a) I show tough love and emphasize obedience (Authoritarian)

b) I balance warmth with clear expectations (Authoritative)

c) I prioritize warmth and acceptance (Permissive)

d) Emotional support isn't a focus for me (Uninvolved)

2. What's your response when your child makes a mistake?

a) Apply strict consequences to ensure they learn (Authoritarian)

b) Discuss the mistake and guide them toward a solution (Authoritative)

c) Be understanding and forgiving (Permissive)

d) Let them handle it independently (Uninvolved)

3. How do you communicate with your child?

a) Communication is directive, emphasizing obedience (Authoritarian)

b) I encourage open communication with clear expectations (Authoritative)

c) I foster open dialogue, even if it challenges rules (Permissive)

d) Communication is not a priority for me (Uninvolved)

Scoring:

Mostly As: Authoritarian Parenting Style

Mostly Bs: Authoritative Parenting Style

Mostly Cs: Permissive Parenting Style

Mostly Ds: Uninvolved Parenting Style

Keep track of your answers and refer to the descriptions in the earlier chapter to learn more about your predominant parenting style. Remember, every parent is unique, and this quiz is just a tool to help you understand your general approach.

As we conclude this chapter, it's clear that no single parenting style defines the perfect approach. Each style brings its strengths and challenges, shaping the way we guide and nurture our children. Understanding these different approaches allows us to reflect on our own parenting methods and make intentional choices that align with our values and our children's needs. The key lies in balance—finding a way to provide structure while fostering independence, and offering warmth while maintaining clear boundaries.

CHAPTER 5: STRIKING THE BALANCE: THE ART OF PARENTING

In this chapter, we examine the delicate balance between strict parenting and indulgence, highlighting the profound influence of words on a child's growth. We explore how the way we communicate with young minds—whether through discipline or affection—shapes their emotional development, self-esteem, and worldview. By understanding the power of language, we uncover the lasting impact it has on their future well-being and behaviour.

Each and Every Word Has Power:

"Each word carries weight and leaves a lasting impression." This mantra serves as a guiding principle for parents as they navigate the intricate landscape of raising children. The language we choose shapes the environment we create for our young ones.

By surrounding them with powerful, spiritual, loving, and health-focused words, we contribute to their overall wellness and effortless growth.

Example:

Parents consciously incorporate positive affirmations into daily conversations, reinforcing confidence, gratitude, bliss, and peace. Words such as strength, belief, honesty, care, happiness, and kindness become the building blocks of a nurturing atmosphere.

Children Learn by Observation:

Children are keen observers; they absorb the essence of their surroundings. Instead of solely relying on verbal teachings, parents must embody the morals, values, and ideologies they wish to impart. The creation of a loving environment becomes the foundation for a child's natural joyfulness.

Example:

In a household where parents consistently display kindness, genuine care, and happiness, children naturally emulate these qualities. The atmosphere at home becomes a reflection of consistent positive demonstrations.

Maintaining a Joyful Atmosphere:

It's crucial for parents to create an environment where anxiety, fear, anger, frustration, and resentment are minimal. By maintaining a household filled with joy and love, parents guarantee a conducive space for their children to grow up well-adjusted.

Example:

A consistent demonstration of a wonderful life by parents becomes the blueprint for a pleasant and harmonious home. External influences may pose challenges, but children raised in a positive environment possess the resilience to navigate and overcome adversities.

Investing in Yourself:

If you want to be an effective parent, you must first invest time and effort in your own personal growth. Take a moment to reflect—do you truly understand the essence of education? Are you raising a kind, thoughtful human being, or simply molding your child to fit society's expectations? The choice is yours.

Think about it—when you work on yourself, challenge your own beliefs, and commit to personal growth, you become a living example for your child. Instead of just telling them what to do, you show them through your actions. The focus isn't on shaping them alone but on becoming the kind of person you hope they will emulate. Be the role model they deserve.

Here are some simple yet meaningful ways to spend quality time with your kids:

Nature Outings: Take your child for small outings, treks, or simply enjoy the beauty of nature together.

Physical Activity: Engage in physical activities like playing ball, football, badminton, or passing the parcel to promote good mental and physical health.

Bonding Moments: Share a morning walk with your child, fostering a strong bond while enhancing physical and mental well-being.

Outdoor Adventures: Explore waterparks, gardens, or go for a family morning walk to create memories and promote holistic development.

By investing time in these activities, parents not only contribute to their own well-being but also play an active role in the holistic development of their children.

In essence, parenting is an art that requires continual self-improvement, conscious language choices, and meaningful interactions. Striking the right balance between being a guide and fostering independence is key to raising well-rounded and resilient individuals.

Weekend Event Planner for Quality Time with Your Young Ones

Planning intentional and enjoyable weekends with your children strengthens your bond, creates lasting memories, and provides opportunities for learning and fun. This exercise will help you design a weekend itinerary that balances structured activities with free time, ensuring a fulfilling experience for both you and your children.

Sample Weekend Event Planner

Saturday

- **9:00 AM – 10:30 AM: Outdoor Adventure**

  o **Activity:** Nature hike or a visit to the local park.

  o **Objective:** Encourage physical activity and exploration of nature.

  o **Materials Needed:** Comfortable clothing, snacks, and water.

- **10:30 AM – 12:00 PM: Creative Play**

  o **Activity:** Arts and crafts session at home.

  o **Objective:** Foster creativity and fine motor skills.

- o **Materials Needed:** Paper, markers, paints, glue, and craft supplies.

- **12:00 PM – 1:00 PM: Lunch**

  - o **Activity:** Prepare and enjoy a family picnic.

  - o **Objective:** Encourage healthy eating and family bonding.

  - o **Materials Needed:** Picnic basket, blanket, and lunch items.

- **1:00 PM – 3:00 PM: Learning Activity**

  - o **Activity:** Visit a local museum or science center.

  - o **Objective:** Promote learning and curiosity.

  - o **Materials Needed:** Tickets, comfortable walking shoes.

- **3:00 PM – 5:00 PM: Free Time**

  - o **Activity:** Playtime at home or a quiet reading session.

  - o **Objective:** Allow for relaxation and personal interests.

  - o **Materials Needed:** Toys, books, or games.

- 5:00 PM – 6:30 PM: Family Dinner

  o **Activity:** Cook a meal together and enjoy family conversation.

  o **Objective:** Encourage teamwork and communication.

  o **Materials Needed:** Ingredients for dinner, cooking utensils.

- 6:30 PM – 8:00 PM: Movie Night

  o **Activity:** Watch a family-friendly movie at home.

  o **Objective:** Provide a relaxed end to the day.

  o **Materials Needed:** Movie, popcorn, and cozy blankets.

Sunday

- 9:00 AM – 10:30 AM: Sports and Games

  o **Activity:** Play a family game of soccer or a fun sport.

  o **Objective:** Promote physical fitness and teamwork.

  o **Materials Needed:** Sports equipment.

- **10:30 AM – 12:00 PM: Baking Together**

  o **Activity:** Bake cookies or cupcakes as a family.

  o **Objective:** Teach cooking skills and enjoy a sweet treat.

  o **Materials Needed:** Baking ingredients and utensils.

- **12:00 PM – 1:00 PM: Lunch**

  o **Activity:** Enjoy a casual lunch at a favorite spot or at home.

  o **Objective:** Relax and enjoy time together.

  o **Materials Needed:** Lunch items or dining out.

- **1:00 PM – 3:00 PM: Outdoor Play**

  o **Activity:** Visit a playground or have a family bike ride.

  o **Objective:** Encourage active play and exploration.

  o **Materials Needed:** Bicycles, helmets, or playground equipment.

- **3:00 PM – 4:00 PM: Educational Fun**

  o **Activity:** Engage in a science experiment or educational game at home.

- o **Objective:** Foster learning through play.

- o **Materials Needed:** Science kit or educational toys.

- **4:00 PM – 5:00 PM: Family Meeting**

  - o **Activity:** Plan and discuss upcoming activities or reflect on the weekend.

  - o **Objective:** Promote communication and planning skills.

  - o **Materials Needed:** Notepad and pen for notes.

- **5:00 PM – 6:00 PM: Dinner Prep**

  - o **Activity:** Prepare a simple meal together or have a family cook-off.

  - o **Objective:** Encourage teamwork and culinary skills.

  - o **Materials Needed:** Ingredients and cooking utensils.

- **6:00 PM – 7:00 PM: Relaxation Time**

  - o **Activity:** Enjoy a calming activity such as a family walk or relaxation exercises.

  - o **Objective:** Wind down and prepare for the week ahead.

o **Materials Needed:** Comfortable clothing for a walk or relaxation tools.

By thoughtfully planning your weekends with a mix of engaging activities and downtime, you can create meaningful experiences that strengthen family bonds and enrich your children's lives. Enjoy your time together and embrace the joy of shared adventures!

CHAPTER 6: HEALING THE INNER CHILD: BECOMING THE PARENT YOU ASPIRE TO BE

Inner child healing is a therapeutic process that involves addressing and nurturing the wounded aspects of oneself that originated from childhood experiences. The "inner child" refers to the emotional and psychological residue of childhood, including both positive and negative imprints. This concept suggests that the experiences and emotions we encounter during our early years can significantly influence our thoughts, behaviours, and relationships in adulthood.

Understanding and healing our inner child is a profound and transformative journey that holds immense significance in the realm of parenting. Delving into the recesses of our own childhood experiences allows us to uncover unresolved emotions, unmet needs, and ingrained patterns of behaviour that may unknowingly influence our approach to parenting. By acknowledging and addressing these aspects of our inner child, we equip ourselves with a heightened capacity for empathy, patience, and authentic connection with our own children.

Inner child healing matters for parenting because it provides an opportunity to break free from the cycles of generational patterns and negative influences that may have shaped our own upbringing. By nurturing and healing our inner child, we gain a deeper understanding of the wounds that may impact our parenting style, allowing us to consciously choose a different path for our children.

Moreover, healing our inner child is pivotal for cultivating emotional resilience and responsiveness. It enables us to recognize and appropriately address our own triggers, preventing the unintentional projection of unresolved emotions onto our children. Through this process, we become better equipped to provide a safe and nurturing environment for our children to express themselves, fostering open communication and trust.

During my journey of inner child healing, I uncovered a wound I hadn't fully healed from—the loss of my grandmother. I was 17 when she crossed over, and though time moved forward, a part of me remained frozen in that grief.

We shared countless small but precious moments—she would gently towel-dry my hair, spread an extra bit of butter on my bread because she knew I loved it, or peel groundnuts for me while we watched my favourite cartoon. These simple gestures were woven into the fabric of my childhood, filling my world with warmth and unconditional love.

Her passing left an emptiness I struggled to process. For nearly a year and a half, a cloud of sorrow followed me. I didn't smile the way I used to. I had lost not just my grandmother but my epitome of love—the one who made the ordinary feel extraordinary.

Healing meant revisiting that pain, allowing myself to grieve fully, and embracing the love she left behind. In doing so, I realized that love never truly leaves us; it transforms, becoming a guiding light within.

Techniques of Inner Child Healing That Helped Me Overcome My Grandmother's Death

1. Reparenting My Inner Child

For years, a part of me—the 17-year-old girl who lost her grandmother—remained stuck in sorrow. She needed comfort, reassurance, and love, but I had never permitted myself to grieve fully. Through reparenting, I learned to nurture that part of me.

I would sit in quiet reflection, close my eyes, and visualize myself as a teenager. I would speak to her with kindness, saying things like:

"I know this hurts. I know you miss her deeply. But she hasn't truly left you. She lives in every memory; in every habit she passed down to you. You are safe, and it's okay to smile again."

This practice allowed me to become the source of comfort I once sought from my grandmother. Slowly, I began to feel a sense of peace, knowing that the love we shared was still a part of me.

2. Creating a Ritual to Honor Her Memory

One of the hardest parts of grief is the feeling that we are leaving our loved ones behind. I struggled with the idea that life was moving forward without my grandmother physically present. To heal, I created a ritual of remembrance—a way to celebrate her presence in my life rather than mourn her absence.

Every year on her birthday, I light a candle, sit with her favourite cup of tea, and write her a letter. In these letters, I tell her about my life, my achievements, and even my struggles. It makes me feel connected to her as if she is still guiding me.

Over time, this practice transformed my grief. Instead of feeling like I had lost her, I began to feel her presence in the small, everyday moments—the way I still love extra butter on my bread or how the scent of fresh groundnuts reminds me of our time together.

As parents engage in inner child healing, they often experience a profound shift in perspective, viewing both themselves and their children through a lens of compassion and understanding. This newfound self-awareness allows for greater patience, empathy, and flexibility in navigating the challenges of parenthood. It offers an opportunity to rewrite the narrative of our own childhood, creating a positive and empowering legacy for the next generation.

Inner child healing is not just a personal journey; it's an investment in the well-being of our families.

By consciously tending to the needs of our inner child, we unlock the potential for more authentic connections with our children, creating a ripple effect of healing that transcends generations. In recognizing the importance of inner child healing for parenting, we embark on a transformative journey that shapes not only our narrative but also the narrative of the family we are nurturing.

Having grasped the importance of inner child healing, let's delve into the various facets that may have played a role in shaping it.

Breaking Generational Patterns:

Unresolved issues from childhood can lead to the unintentional perpetuation of negative patterns in parenting. Inner child healing provides an opportunity to break these generational cycles, fostering a healthier family environment.

Understanding Triggers and Reactions:

By exploring and healing the wounds of the inner child, parents gain insight into their triggers and reactions. This self-awareness enables them to respond to their children with greater empathy and patience.

Enhancing Emotional Availability:

Childhood wounds can affect emotional availability. Inner child healing allows parents to address emotional blockages and become more emotionally present for their children, fostering a deeper connection.

Improving Communication:

Unhealed wounds can impact communication styles. Inner child healing helps parents recognize and transform communication patterns, creating a more open and supportive dialogue with their children.

Promoting Self-Compassion:

Inner child healing involves self-compassion and self-nurturing. When parents learn to care for their own inner child, they are better equipped to extend that compassion to their children, creating a more nurturing family dynamic.

Reducing Stress and Anxiety:

Childhood traumas and unmet needs can contribute to stress and anxiety in adulthood. Inner child healing aims to alleviate these burdens, allowing parents to approach their role with a greater sense of calm and resilience.

Building Resilience in Children:

As parents heal their own inner child, they model resilience for their children. This, in turn, helps the younger generation develop emotional strength and coping mechanisms to navigate life's challenges.

Creating a Loving Environment:

Inner child healing contributes to the creation of a loving and supportive home environment. When parents address their wounds, they are better able to provide the warmth and security essential for a child's healthy development.

By tending to your inner child, parents lay the foundation for conscious and mindful parenting, fostering healthier relationships and nurturing an environment where children can thrive emotionally, socially, and psychologically.

Inner Child Healing Assignment: Identifying Traits and Healing Approaches

Objective: To explore and identify specific traits or patterns from your childhood that may require healing and to formulate a personalized approach for inner child healing.

Instructions:

Reflect on Childhood Traits: Take dedicated time for self-reflection. Consider your own childhood experiences and identify specific traits, behaviours, or patterns that you believe may stem from unresolved issues.

Few sample Traits:

Difficulty expressing emotions

Fear of failure

Perfectionism

Difficulty setting boundaries

Low self-esteem

Write a life event where you experienced this:

____

____

____

____

____

____

____

____

Create a list detailing the identified traits. Be honest and specific about how these traits manifest in your adult life and parenting style.

Example:

Trait: Difficulty expressing emotions

Manifestation: Tendency to avoid emotional conversations, struggles with vulnerability.

Select Healing Approaches:

For each identified trait, choose a healing approach or practice that resonates with you. Consider techniques such as therapy, self-help exercises, or mindfulness practices.

Example Healing Approaches:

Trait: Difficulty expressing emotions

Healing Approach: Engage in journaling, practice mindful breathing to connect with emotions, and consider seeking therapy to explore underlying issues.

Formulate an Action Plan:

Develop a personalized action plan that outlines how you will integrate the chosen healing approaches into your daily life.

Example Action Plan:

Trait: Difficulty expressing emotions

Action Plan:

Journal for 15 minutes each day to explore and process emotions.

Practice mindful breathing exercises during moments of emotional tension.

Schedule a consultation with a therapist to delve deeper into emotional expression challenges.

Set Realistic Goals:

Establish achievable goals for implementing your action plan. Break down the steps and commit to gradual progress.

Example Goals:

Week 1: Begin daily journaling for at least 10 minutes.

Week 2: Integrate mindful breathing exercises into morning routine.

Week 4: Schedule initial therapy consultation.

Regular Self-Check-ins:

Schedule regular self-check-ins to assess your progress. Reflect on any changes in the identified traits and adjust your approach if needed.

Celebrate Milestones:

Acknowledge and celebrate milestones in your healing journey. Recognize the positive changes and growth, no matter how small.

Example Milestones:

Successfully journaled for a month.

Engaged in therapy sessions consistently for three months.

This assignment is designed to guide you through a thoughtful exploration of your inner child and to provide actionable steps for healing. Remember, the goal is progress, not perfection. Embrace the journey with compassion, and celebrate the transformative power of self-discovery and healing.

As we conclude this chapter, I extend my heartfelt congratulations on your remarkable journey. Your resilience and commitment shine brightly. Now, let us embark on an exploration together, delving into the profound significance of attending to your child's emotional needs.

CHAPTER 7: UNLOCKING HEARTS: WHY YOUR CHILD'S VOICE MATTERS

As a parenting coach, I frequently hear from concerned parents about the shifting nature of communication with their children. The once open channels seem to close, and with that comes the familiar question: "They used to share everything, but now they've stopped. Why?"

This shift is not uncommon, as even renowned thinkers have pointed to the complexities of growing up.

As the poet William Wordsworth wisely noted, "The childhood shows the man, as morning shows the day." Children evolve, and with that evolution comes a change in how they relate to the world and to us.

Similarly, as the famous child psychologist Jean Piaget observed, "The principal goal of education is to create men who are capable of doing new things, not simply repeating what other generations have done."

In this chapter, we explore how these changes in communication are part of a natural developmental process, and how parents can navigate this shift to maintain connection during the challenging yet transformative years of adolescence.

The Shift in Communication:

Remember the early years when your child eagerly shared every detail of their day, from the minutiae of school activities to the joyous escapades with friends? What changed? Why did the once-open communication channel seem to close?

The Power of Acceptance:

Children crave acceptance. When they were younger, your positive response to their tales brought joy and validation. However, as they grew older, a shift occurred. Perhaps your reaction to certain events conveyed disapproval, disappointment, or anger.

Rejection and Its Consequences:

The pivotal moment comes when a child, seeking acceptance, is met with rejection. It might be a minor incident like bunking classes for a quick snack or going to a movie. Instead of acknowledgment and understanding, they face criticism or disapproval.

The Ripple Effect:

With each rejection, the child internalizes the message: "If I'm honest, I'll face anger or disappointment." The natural response? They begin to withhold information. It's not that they've stopped engaging in activities; they've stopped sharing them with you.

Nurturing an Open Channel:

To foster open communication, it's crucial to shift your response from judgment to understanding. For instance, when faced with a revelation about a McDonald's escapade or a movie, consider responding with empathy and curiosity rather than criticism.

Let's look at a Constructive Approach:

Instead of:

"What were you thinking?"

"Did I raise you to behave this way?"

"Wasting my hard-earned money!"

Try:

"How do you feel about it?"

"I understand, but let's talk about it."

"Next time, let's plan better. Take extra money for popcorn."

The Role of Unconditional Acceptance:

Children find solace in environments where they are unconditionally accepted. If they fear judgment or criticism, they'll seek out alternative sources of support, like school counsellors.

Bridging the Gap:

Understanding the difference between a counsellor and a parent is crucial. A counsellor offers a non-judgmental space, but a parent can provide love, care, protection, and blessings. The challenge? To become a parent-counsellor, offering both understanding and unwavering support.

The Need for Unconditional Love:

In today's world, where myriad influences shape your child's experiences, the key to their protection is maintaining an open line of communication. If they feel safe sharing every aspect of their lives, they are more likely to turn to you for guidance and support.

Your child is not wrong; they are navigating a complex world, seeking understanding and acceptance. By fostering open communication and embracing unconditional love, you become not just a parent but a trusted confidant in their journey through life.

It's Difficult, but Not Impossible: The Art of Self-Healing and Strengthening Relationships

As a parenting expert, I often emphasize the interconnectedness of personal well-being and the health of relationships, especially within the context of marriage. In this chapter, we delve into the transformative power of self-healing and explore how it contributes to the enrichment and improvement of marital bonds.

The Six Steps of Self-Healing:

Understanding the Power of Self-Healing: Acknowledge that self-healing is a journey that requires conscious effort.

Embracing Emotional Intelligence: Develop emotional intelligence to navigate challenges effectively.

Cultivating Mindfulness: Practice mindfulness to stay present and attuned to your emotions.

Forgiveness and Letting Go: Release resentment and embrace forgiveness for emotional freedom.

Nurturing Physical Well-being: Recognize the connection between physical health and emotional balance.

Cultivating Healthy Relationships: Foster positive relationships to create a supportive network.

Nurturing Marital Intimacy:

Contrary to common belief, intimacy is not just about physical closeness but involves a deep understanding and acceptance between partners. Drawing from the example of Prince Charles, who faced challenges in his marriage, the chapter emphasizes that the foundation of a happy marriage is built on emotional intimacy.

Tips for a Healthy Husband-Wife Relationship:

Create a Comfortable Space: Foster an environment where you both feel comfortable and present for each other.

Silent Connection: Engage in silent moments of togetherness, holding hands, and cuddling.

Escape Life's Ups and Downs: During difficult times, focus on the present and reminisce about sweet memories.

Privacy Within the Relationship: Keep discussions between the two of you, avoiding involvement of friends or family.

Take Walks Together: Physical activity can aid discussions and prevent unnecessary debates.

Never Stop Dating: Keep the romance alive by planning date nights, even as the years go by.

Actions Speak Louder Than Words: Express love through caring gestures, thoughtful actions, and surprise gifts.

Revitalizing Relationships through Gratitude:

Introducing a gratitude exercise, the chapter underscores the importance of acknowledging the positive aspects of life. The exercise involves listing desires on one side and expressing gratitude for current blessings on the other.

Aura and Physical Closeness:

Highlighting the concept of auras, the chapter suggests that prolonged physical separation can negatively impact the compatibility of a marriage. Encouraging physical closeness, the text argues that frequent contact enhances the complementary nature of a couple's energy fields.

Three Rules for a Lasting Relationship:

Avoid Unwarranted Criticism: Never make your partner feel unappreciated or undesired.

No Cheating: In the face of challenges, maintain faithfulness.

Support Through Thick and Thin: Always have your partner's back through the good and bad times.

The GRG Exercise:

Gratitude is promoted as a tool for enriching life and relationships. The GRG (Gratitude Reflection and Growth) exercise involves listing things desired and expressing gratitude for current blessings, fostering a positive mindset.

While acknowledging the difficulties, the chapter emphasizes that a thriving marriage is not an impossible feat. By incorporating self-healing practices, nurturing intimacy, and expressing gratitude, couples can fortify their bonds and enjoy enduring, fulfilling relationships. The chapter closes with a powerful quote by Mitesh Khatri, urging individuals to be grateful for what they have, ensuring a continuous cycle of abundance and appreciation.

CHAPTER 08: LISTENING MATTERS: UNLOCKING THE POWER OF YOUR CHILD'S VOICE

In the intricate tapestry of parenting, one thread stands out prominently—the power of words. The impact of language on a child's emotional well-being and future cannot be overstated.

This chapter delves into the transformative influence of words, weaving a narrative around the life of one of history's greatest inventors, Thomas Edison.

Thomas Edison: A Tale of Transformational Vocabulary

Thomas Edison, born on February 11, 1847, emerged from an ordinary childhood with extraordinary potential. A pivotal moment occurred when Edison, carrying a letter from his teacher, approached his mother. The contents of that letter, filled with encouragement and foresight, set the stage for Edison's transformative journey.

"Your son is a genius; this school is too small for him," read the letter from the principal. In response to such affirming words, Edison's mother took on the responsibility of homeschooling him. Throughout his lifetime, Edison secured 1,093 patents, cementing his legacy as a prolific inventor.

.However, fate took a curious turn when Edison, sifting through family memorabilia, discovered another letter. This one, tucked away in a drawer, bore a different message:

"Your son is addled; we won't let him come to school anymore." The revelation brought Edison to tears, yet he declared in his diary that he was an adult child raised by a hero mother, ultimately becoming the genius of the century.

Parental Impact on a Child's Foundation

Edison's story serves as a powerful testament to the influence parents wield in shaping a child's foundational beliefs.

The words spoken, both positive and negative, reverberate through the corridors of their minds, guiding the trajectory of their lives.

The Beauty of Transformational Vocabulary

Recognizing the power of positive language is essential in parenting. The chapter emphasizes that words are not mere tools of communication but instruments that have the power to shape beliefs and actions.

The concept is presented as a simple yet universally applicable tool that can immediately enhance the quality of life for both parent and child.

Negative Labels and Their Impact

The text underscores the detrimental effect of negative labels on a child's psyche. Words such as "lazy," "lack of discipline," or "selfish" become self-fulfilling prophecies, shaping a child's identity and behaviour. The call to replace these negative labels with positive affirmations is an invitation to cultivate an environment where a child's self-image flourishes.

Assignment: A Path to Upliftment

A practical assignment is offered to parents—to replace negative words with positive ones. This simple exercise aims to rewire thought patterns, fostering positivity and empowerment.

The science behind the assignment lies in creating consistent positive associations between thoughts and emotions in the brain.

Mixed Neuro Associations: The Science Behind It

The concept of mixed neuro associations is introduced, urging parents to align their thoughts and words positively. The chapter provides insight into the neurological links between thoughts and emotions, emphasizing the need to avoid mixed messages for desired positive outcomes.

Affirmations:

As a parent, you have the unique opportunity to shape your child's self-esteem and emotional well-being, and one of the simplest yet most powerful ways to do this is through affirmations. By offering positive, encouraging statements, you can help your child build confidence, resilience, and a healthy sense of self. Whether your little one is just beginning to explore the world or navigating the complexities of adolescence, affirmations can be tailored to support their growth at every stage. In this chapter, I'll introduce you to affirmations that align with your child's age and developmental needs, giving you a valuable tool to nurture their emotional and mental well-being while reinforcing a positive mindset that lasts a lifetime.

Here are some affirmations for parents to use with their children, focusing on overall development for each age group. These affirmations are inspired by child development research and can be personalized to fit your child's needs.

0-3 Years:

"You are safe, loved, and cherished every day."

"You are curious and brave, exploring the world around you."

"Your smile brings joy to everyone around you."

"You are growing strong and healthy every day."

"You are special, and the world is a better place with you in it."

3-5 Years:

"You are a kind and loving friend."

"You are strong, and you can handle anything that comes your way."

"You are smart, and you learn new things every day."

"Your imagination is wonderful, and your ideas are valuable."

"You are important, and your voice matters."

5-10 Years:

"You are capable of great things and can achieve your goals."

"You are a problem solver, and you can find solutions to challenges."

"You are proud of yourself, and your hard work pays off."

"You are unique, and there is no one else like you."

"You are kind and treat others with respect and care."

10-15 Years:

"You are strong and can face challenges with courage."

"You trust yourself to make wise decisions and follow your heart."

"You are worthy of love and respect, just as you are."

"You have the power to create the future you dream of."

"You are proud of who you are and the person you are becoming."

15-18 Years:

"You are in charge of your destiny, and your future is bright."

"You are capable of overcoming obstacles and growing stronger."

"You are unique, and you embrace your individuality with confidence."

"You trust in your abilities and believe in your dreams."

"You are enough, and you have everything you need to succeed."

Consider creating personalized affirmations that align with your child's unique developmental journey. These personalized, positive statements can serve as powerful tools to support their growth, build confidence, and inspire them to reach their full potential.

1.

2.

3.

4.

5.

CHAPTER 9: BEHAVIOUR MODELLING - A BLUEPRINT FOR EFFECTIVE PARENTING

Parenting is a nuanced art—a dance where every step leaves an indelible mark on a child's developing personality.

In this chapter, we delve into the profound influence of behaviour modelling, recognizing it as a powerful tool that shapes the future of our children.

The Profound Impact of Behaviour Modelling

"Children learn more from what you are than what you teach."— W. E. B. Du BoisIndeed, the power of behaviour modelling is unparalleled.

Children are keen observers, absorbing not just explicit lessons but also the implicit messages embedded in everyday actions. As parents, our behaviours become the blueprint that shapes their understanding of the world.

Whether we are conscious of it or not, our children watch, learn, and imitate. This unconscious mirroring of parental behaviour is a natural part of the developmental process.

Therefore, parents must be intentional about the behaviours they model.

Observational Learning in Children

Observational learning, also known as imitation or modelling, is a fundamental aspect of childhood development. Children learn not just from direct interactions but also from observing others, especially their primary caregivers. Behaviour modelling encompasses a wide range of actions, from simple politeness to complex conflict resolution.

Politeness Matters: Saying "Thank You" and "Please. "Simple acts of politeness leave a lasting impression. Saying "thank you" and "please" not only teaches manners but also instills the importance of gratitude and respect.

Sharing as a Learned Behaviour Children can be naturally possessive. Modelling sharing—whether it's a book, a meal, or attention—lays the foundation for generosity and communal living.

Conflict Resolution: Calm Communication Over Shouting Conflict is inevitable, whether between siblings or friends.

By modelling calm communication during disagreements, parents provide a template for effective problem-solving. The tone set in these moments becomes an emotional compass for the child.

Understanding Modelling as a Learning Mechanism

Modelling is more than mimicry; it is a profound form of observational learning. From tying shoelaces to problem-solving, children internalize behaviours through observation. This mechanism helps them develop essential life skills and a sense of reasoning.

Effective Parenting: Encouraging Positive Habits

Effective parenting extends beyond discouraging undesirable habits—it involves actively encouraging positive behaviours.

A parent's role is not just that of a rule-setter but also a role model and guide.

Teaching Love, Responsibility, and Healthy Living

Parenting requires a multifaceted approach. Teaching children about love, responsibility, and healthy living goes beyond verbal instruction. Children must witness these values in action to internalize them.

Character Building Through Modelling

Character building is an ongoing process closely tied to behaviour modelling. The traits we exemplify—integrity, empathy, resilience—become the building blocks of our children's character.

Time Investment: A Testament to Priorities

Being a good role model demands an investment of time. In a world saturated with distractions, allocating quality time to our children communicates that they are a priority. In these moments, they learn about love, values, and their own self-worth.

Guidance with Love and Affection: The Ideal Parenting Approach

Guidance is not synonymous with dictation. The most effective guidance is delivered with love and affection, balancing boundaries with a sense of autonomy.

Nurturing Confidence: Cultivating Self-Esteem

Praising a child's achievements and actions may seem simple, but its impact on self-esteem is profound. Positive reinforcement fosters a child's belief in their abilities and strengthens their self-image.

By intentionally demonstrating positive behaviours, parents contribute to their children's emotional well-being and character development.

Instilling Positive Behaviours in Toddlers

Identify Simple Behaviours: Focus on age-appropriate behaviours such as kindness, sharing, and basic manners.

Use Visual Cues: Toddlers respond well to visual aids like picture charts or storybooks to reinforce positive behaviours. For example, use visuals showing happy faces when they share toys.

Celebrate Small Victories: Toddlers thrive on positive reinforcement. Praise even the smallest instances of good behaviour to encourage repetition.

Be Consistent: Consistency is key when modelling behaviours for toddlers. Repetition helps them internalize positive habits.

Incorporate Play: Use playtime to model positive behaviours. Role-playing scenarios can help toddlers learn through imitation.

Establish a Routine: Create routines that include specific times for practicing positive behaviours, such as sharing toys or expressing gratitude. Predictable routines reinforce learning.

Behaviour Modelling for Teenagers

Engage in Open Discussions: Communicate with teenagers about the values and behaviours you wish to model. Encourage them to share their perspectives.

Model Effective Communication: Active listening, respectful disagreement, and assertive expression are crucial skills that parents should exemplify.

Joint Problem-Solving: Involve teenagers in collaborative problem-solving scenarios, emphasizing compromise and empathy.

Demonstrate Emotional Regulation: Teenagers often struggle with emotional control. Model healthy emotional regulation by expressing feelings constructively and managing stress positively.

Encourage Independence: Model responsible decision-making by allowing teenagers to witness thoughtful choices and accountability in action.

Showcase Lifelong Learning: Exhibit a growth mindset by demonstrating curiosity, adaptability, and a willingness to learn from mistakes.

Assignment Reflection

1. Journal Reflection:

Maintain a journal to document your experiences with behaviour modelling for toddlers and teenagers. Record specific behaviours, challenges, and improvements.

2. Family Discussion:

Engage your family in discussions about behaviour modelling. Encourage open communication where each member shares their observations, feedback, and thoughts.

3. Adaptation Strategies:

Identify which strategies worked well and which need adjustments. Adapt your approach based on the unique needs and responses of your children.

This assignment provides an opportunity to tailor behaviour modelling to the distinct developmental stages of toddlers and teenagers.

By focusing on age-appropriate behaviours and refining your approach, you significantly contribute to your children's positive development. The reflection and discussion components serve as valuable tools for continuous improvement within your family dynamics.

CHAPTER 10: TECHNOLOGY AND PARENTING: NURTURING HEALTHY DIGITAL HABITS IN A TECH-DRIVEN WORLD

In the contemporary landscape, technology is an omnipresent force, influencing every facet of our lives. For parents raising children in a tech-driven world, understanding the impact of technology on child development and cultivating healthy digital habits is paramount.

This chapter delves into the multifaceted relationship between parenting and technology, offering insights, strategies, and guidelines for fostering a balanced and mindful approach.

The digital landscape has rapidly evolved, bringing both opportunities and challenges for parents. Children today are digital natives, growing up in a world where smartphones, tablets, and the internet are integral aspects of daily life.

As parents, comprehending this digital milieu is crucial for effectively guiding our children through its complexities.

Key Aspects of the Digital Landscape:

Digital Literacy: The ability to use technology effectively and responsibly is a vital skill. Parents play a pivotal role in imparting digital literacy to their children.

Online Communication: Social media platforms, messaging apps, and online forums have become primary modes of communication for children. Understanding these mediums is essential for parents to ensure safe online interactions.

Educational Technology: Technology is increasingly integrated into educational settings. Recognizing the benefits and potential drawbacks of educational technology is essential for informed decision-making.

Entertainment and Screen Time: The pervasive nature of screens in daily life raises concerns about excessive screen time and its impact on children's well-being. Striking a balance between technology use and other activities is a crucial parental responsibility.

Establishing Healthy Screen Time Guidelines

The American Academy of Pediatrics recommends that children aged 2 to 5 should have no more than one hour of screen time per day, while children aged 6 and older should have consistent limits on the amount of screen time they engage in. However, creating effective screen time guidelines goes beyond mere time constraints; it involves fostering a holistic approach to technology use.

Components of Healthy Screen Time Guidelines:

Age-Appropriate Content: Ensure that the content your child engages with is age-appropriate and aligns with your family values.

Balanced Activities: Encourage a mix of activities beyond screens, such as outdoor play, reading, and creative pursuits.

Family Media Use Plan: Collaboratively develop a family media use plan that includes designated screen-free times and zones.

Modelling Healthy Habits: Children often model their behaviour on their parents. Demonstrating healthy screen habits sets a positive example.

Promoting Digital Literacy

Digital literacy is more than just knowing how to use technology; it encompasses critical thinking, ethical decision-making, and responsible online behaviour. Parents play a pivotal role in nurturing digital literacy skills in their children.

Strategies for Promoting Digital Literacy:

Open Dialogue: Foster open conversations about the digital world, addressing topics such as online safety, privacy, and the consequences of digital actions.

Educational Apps and Games: Integrate educational apps and games that promote learning while engaging children in a positive digital environment.

Teaching Critical Evaluation: Help children critically evaluate online content, discerning between reliable and unreliable sources.

Setting Boundaries: Establish clear boundaries on the types of online activities that are permissible, taking into account age appropriateness and individual maturity.

Online Safety and Cybersecurity:

The online world presents potential risks, including cyberbullying, inappropriate content, and privacy concerns. Safeguarding children in the digital realm requires a proactive and informed approach to online safety.

Key Aspects of Online Safety:

Privacy Settings: Regularly review and set privacy settings on devices and social media accounts to control the amount of personal information shared online.

Cyberbullying Awareness: Educate children about cyberbullying, emphasizing the importance of reporting any instances and seeking support.

Open Communication: Establish an environment where children feel comfortable discussing their online experiences and concerns without fear of punishment.

Supervision and Monitoring: While respecting a child's need for autonomy, maintaining age-appropriate supervision and monitoring is crucial for ensuring online safety.

Balancing Educational Technology

Educational technology has become a staple in many classrooms, offering interactive and engaging learning experiences.

However, striking a balance between the benefits and potential drawbacks of educational technology is essential for parents.

Guidelines for Balancing Educational Technology:

Quality over Quantity: Prioritize high-quality educational content that aligns with your child's developmental stage and academic needs.

Active Involvement: Stay actively involved in your child's educational technology use, understanding the platforms and apps they engage with.

Supplement with Offline Learning: Balance digital learning with traditional offline activities to provide a comprehensive educational experience.

Regular Assessments: Periodically assess the impact of educational technology on your child's learning outcomes and overall well-being.

Cultivating Mindful Tech Use

Mindful technology use involves being intentional, present, and aware of the impact of digital interactions on well-being. Instilling a sense of mindfulness in children sets the foundation for a healthy relationship with technology.

Strategies for Cultivating Mindful Tech Use:

Tech-Free Zones: Designate specific areas or times in your home where technology is not allowed, promoting face-to-face interactions and relaxation.

Digital Detox: Periodically engage in digital detoxes as a family, encouraging activities that do not involve screens.

Role Modelling: Demonstrate mindful tech use by being present during family time, meals, and conversations.

Encouraging Outdoor Activities: Promote outdoor play and physical activities to counterbalance sedentary screen time.

Addressing Challenges of Parental Control Apps

Parental control apps offer a means of monitoring and restricting a child's online activities. While these tools can be beneficial, they come with their own set of challenges and ethical considerations.

Considerations for Parental Control Apps:

Open Communication: Clearly communicate the purpose of parental control apps to children, emphasizing the importance of online safety.

Balancing Independence: Gradually grant independence as children demonstrate responsible online behaviour, avoiding overly restrictive measures.

Respecting Privacy: Strike a balance between monitoring for safety and respecting a child's need for privacy as they mature.

Education over Control: Prioritize educating children about online risks and responsible behaviour rather than relying solely on restrictive measures.

Building a Supportive Digital Environment

The relationship between parents and technology is symbiotic; as parents navigate the challenges of the digital age, they simultaneously influence their children's attitudes and behaviours.

Creating a supportive digital environment involves collaboration, open communication, and a shared commitment to cultivating positive tech habits.

Building a Supportive Digital Environment:

Family Tech Agreements: Establish clear guidelines through family tech agreements, collaboratively outlining expectations and responsibilities.

Tech Talks: Conduct regular "tech talks" where the family discusses digital trends, emerging technologies, and any concerns or questions.

Parental Education: Stay informed about the latest digital trends and threats, enabling you to guide your children effectively.

Tech-Free Quality Time: Dedicate quality time as a family without the intrusion of technology, fostering stronger interpersonal bonds.

Navigating the intersection of technology and parenting requires continuous adaptation and proactive engagement. A strong commitment to fostering a healthy digital environment is essential.

By understanding the nuances of the digital landscape, implementing mindful tech practices, and prioritizing open communication, parents can empower their children to navigate the digital world with resilience, responsibility, and a strong sense of digital citizenship.

In this era of rapid technological advancement, embracing a thoughtful and informed approach to technology and parenting is not just a choice; it's an imperative for nurturing the well-being and development of the next generation.

CHAPTER 11: PARENTAL SELF-CARE: BALANCING YOUR WELL-BEING FOR EFFECTIVE PARENTING

In the intricate tapestry of parenting, where the threads of love, guidance, and nurture intertwine, one essential strand often overlooked is the well-being of the weaver—the parent. It is imperative to explore the pivotal role of parental self-care in the art of effective parenting.

This chapter delves into the multifaceted aspects of self-care, offering insights, practical strategies, and a nuanced understanding of why prioritizing the well-being of parents is not just a luxury but a necessity for creating a harmonious and thriving family environment.

The Parental Juggling Act: Balancing Responsibilities

Acknowledging the Parental Role

Recognizing the profound impact of parental well-being on the family dynamic

Parents play a crucial role in shaping the family dynamic. Their well-being significantly influences the emotional and physical health of the entire family.

When parents are healthy and happy, they can provide a nurturing and stable environment for their children.

Understanding the various roles parents play and the associated responsibilities

Parents juggle multiple roles, including caregiver, provider, teacher, and role model. Each role comes with its unique set of responsibilities and challenges. Understanding these roles helps parents manage their duties more effectively.

Acknowledging the challenges and rewards that come with the parenting journey

Parenting is a journey filled with both challenges and rewards. Acknowledging the difficulties and celebrating the joys can help parents maintain a balanced perspective.

Parenting Burnout: Signs, Symptoms, and Solutions

Identifying signs of burnout and stress in parents

Burnout is a state of physical, emotional, and mental exhaustion caused by prolonged stress. Signs include irritability, fatigue, and feelings of helplessness. Recognizing these signs early can prevent more serious consequences.

Understanding the physical, emotional, and mental toll of parenting burnout

Burnout affects all aspects of a parent's life, leading to health problems, strained relationships, and decreased effectiveness in parenting. Understanding the toll it takes is the first step in addressing it.

Implementing strategies to prevent and address burnout for sustainable parenting

Preventing burnout involves regular self-care, setting boundaries, and seeking support. When burnout occurs, addressing it promptly through rest, professional help, and lifestyle changes is crucial.

The Essence of Parental Self-Care

Redefining Self-Care for Parents

Shifting Perspectives on Self-Care Beyond Conventional Notions

Self-care is more than spa days and vacations. It includes everyday practices that nurture physical, emotional, and mental health. For parents, this might mean setting aside time for exercise, hobbies, or simply relaxing.

Embracing Self-Care as a Holistic and Ongoing Practice

Self-care is not a one-time activity but a continuous practice. It involves regular check-ins with oneself to ensure needs are being met and making adjustments as necessary.

How Parental Well-Being Enhances Effective Parenting

When parents take care of themselves, they are better equipped to care for their children. This symbiotic relationship means that self-care directly contributes to effective parenting.

Breaking the Guilt Cycle

Addressing the Guilt Associated with Parental Self-Care

Many parents feel guilty about taking time for themselves, believing it detracts from their responsibilities. It's essential to recognize that self-care is not selfish but necessary for sustainable parenting.

Recognizing the Importance of Modelling Self-Compassion for Children

Children learn from their parents' actions. By practicing self-compassion, parents teach their children the value of self-care and self-respect.

Cultivating a Mindset That Prioritizes Both Parental and Child Well-Being

A balanced approach prioritizes both the well-being of the parent and the child. This mindset shift helps create a healthy family dynamic where everyone's needs are valued.

Time Management and Boundaries

Balancing the Demands of Parenting with Personal and Professional Commitments

Effective time management involves prioritizing tasks, delegating when possible, and setting realistic goals. Balancing parenting, personal, and professional commitments requires organization and flexibility.

Setting Realistic Expectations and Establishing Healthy Boundaries

Parents should set realistic expectations for themselves and their children. Establishing boundaries, such as designated work and family times, helps maintain balance.

The Art of Effective Time Management for Parents

Time management techniques, such as using planners, setting priorities, and avoiding overcommitment, can help parents manage their busy schedules more effectively.

Happy parents raise happy children. A joyful home is the best classroom.

Practical Strategies for Parental Self-Care

<u>Physical Well-Being</u>

The Role of Exercise, Nutrition, and Sleep in Parental Self-Care

Regular exercise, balanced nutrition, and sufficient sleep are fundamental to physical well-being. These practices boost energy levels, improve mood, and enhance overall health.

Incorporating Physical Activity into Busy Parenting Routines

Parents can incorporate physical activity by engaging in family exercises, taking walks, or finding short, effective workouts that fit into their schedules.

Prioritizing Sleep Hygiene and Addressing Common Sleep Challenges

Good sleep hygiene involves maintaining a regular sleep schedule, creating a restful environment, and addressing sleep disruptions promptly.

Nurturing Emotional and Mental Health

Recognizing the Emotional Rollercoaster of Parenting

Parenting involves a range of emotions, from joy to frustration. Acknowledging these emotions and finding healthy ways to express and manage them is crucial.

Strategies for Managing Stress, Anxiety, and Parental Overwhelm

Stress management techniques, such as mindfulness, meditation, and deep breathing, can help parents cope with anxiety and overwhelm. Seeking professional support when needed is also vital.

The Importance of Seeking Professional Support When Needed

Therapists, counsellors, and support groups can provide valuable assistance for parents dealing with emotional and mental health challenges.

<u>Building a Support System</u>

Fostering Connections with Other Parents for Mutual Support

Connecting with other parents through playgroups, online forums, or community events provides mutual support and shared experiences.

The Significance of Open Communication with a Partner or Co-Parent

Open communication with a partner or co-parent ensures that parenting responsibilities are shared and support is provided.

Utilizing Community Resources and Seeking Help When Necessary

Community resources, such as parenting classes, childcare services, and support groups, offer additional support for parents.

<u>Carving Out Personal Time</u>

The Importance of Allocating Time for Individual Hobbies and Interests

Engaging in hobbies and interests outside of parenting helps parents maintain a sense of identity and fulfilment.

Strategies for Parents to Maintain a Sense of Identity Beyond Parenting Roles

Parents can maintain their identity by pursuing personal goals, nurturing friendships, and setting aside time for self-reflection.

Incorporating Moments of Solitude and Reflection into Busy Schedules

Finding moments of solitude, whether through meditation, journaling, or quiet reflection, helps parents recharge and gain perspective.

The Impact of Parental Well-Being on Children

<u>Modelling Healthy Habits</u>

The Role of Parents as Primary Influencers in a Child's Life

Children observe and emulate their parents' behaviours. Modelling healthy habits teaches children the importance of self-care and well-being.

Modelling Self-Care as a Valuable Life Skill for Children

By practicing self-care, parents demonstrate its value as a life skill, encouraging children to prioritize their well-being.

Creating a Positive and Nurturing Environment Through Parental Well-Being

A parent's well-being creates a positive and nurturing home environment, fostering the emotional and physical health of the entire family.

<u>Enhancing Parent-Child Relationships</u>

The Correlation Between Parental Happiness and the Quality of Parent-Child Relationships

When parents are happy and healthy, they can form stronger, more positive relationships with their children.

Strategies for Fostering Meaningful Connections with Children Through Self-Care

Spending quality time together, engaging in shared activities, and maintaining open communication enhances parent-child relationships.

Nurturing Open Communication and Emotional Bonds with Children

Encouraging open communication and emotional bonding helps children feel valued and understood.

Cultural and Societal Perspectives on Parental Self-Care

The Cultural Context of Parental Well-Being

Exploring How Cultural Norms and Expectations Impact Parental Self-Care

Cultural norms and expectations can influence how parents perceive and practice self-care. Understanding these influences helps parents navigate them more effectively.

Navigating Cultural Barriers to Self-Care and Well-Being

Addressing cultural barriers involves challenging stereotypes and advocating for the importance of self-care.

Cultivating a Cultural Narrative That Embraces the Importance of Parental Well-Being

Promoting a cultural narrative that values parental well-being encourages broader acceptance and support for self-care practices.

Workplace and Parental Support

Advocating for Workplace Policies That Support Parental Well-Being

Workplace policies, such as flexible hours and parental leave, support parental well-being and work-life balance.

Strategies for Achieving Work-Life Balance and Navigating Parental Leave

Effective strategies include setting boundaries, prioritizing tasks, and advocating for supportive workplace policies.

The Societal Role in Fostering a Culture of Parental Self-Care

Society plays a role in fostering a culture that values and supports parental self-care through policies, resources, and cultural norms.

The Continuum of Parental Self-Care: From Survival to Thriving

Recognizing Different Parenting Seasons

Acknowledging That Parental Self-Care Evolves with Different Life Stages

Parental self-care needs change as children grow and family dynamics shift. Recognizing these changes helps parents adapt their self-care practices.

Strategies for Adapting Self-Care Practices to the Changing Needs of Parents

Flexibility and openness to change are key to adapting self-care practices to meet evolving needs.

The Importance of Flexibility and Self-Compassion in the Self-Care Journey

Flexibility and self-compassion allow parents to navigate the ups and downs of parenting without judgment or guilt.

<u>Fostering a Legacy of Well-Being</u>

The Intergenerational Impact of Parental Self-Care Practices

Parental self-care practices can create a legacy of well-being that influences future generations.

Creating a Legacy of Well-Being That Transcends Generations

By prioritizing self-care, parents set an example for their children and future generations, fostering a culture of health and well-being.

Empowering Parents to Prioritize Self-Care for the Long-Term Health of Their Families

Empowering parents to prioritize self-care ensures the long-term health and happiness of their families, creating a foundation for thriving family dynamics.

Parental self-care is an essential component of effective parenting. By recognizing its importance and implementing practical strategies, parents can create a harmonious and thriving family environment. This chapter aims to empower parents to prioritize their well-being, ensuring they can provide the best care for their children while maintaining their own health and happiness.

DISCLAIMER

The information provided in this book is for general informational and educational purposes only. While the strategies and insights shared in this book are based on research, experience, and best practices in parenting, every child and family is unique. The suggestions provided may not be suitable for every situation, and individual discretion is advised when applying them.

This book is not intended as a substitute for professional advice, whether medical, psychological, or legal. If you have concerns about your child's health, emotional well-being, or any other aspect of their development, please seek guidance from a qualified professional.

The author and publisher disclaim any liability for the use or misuse of the information provided in this book. The reader assumes full responsibility for any choices made based on the content of this book.

Parenting is a journey of love, patience, and learning—take what resonates with you and adapt it to your family's needs.

About The Author

Sanah has been dedicated to the field of education for over a decade. As a high school principal for several years, she has demonstrated exceptional teaching skills and a deep commitment to nurturing young minds. Through her daily interactions with students and parents, she has provided guidance and counselling, helping children enhance their academic performance and strengthening family relationships. Her efforts have not only fostered academic success but have also contributed to happier, healthier family dynamics.

Sanah has positively impacted thousands of students, many of whom have gone on to become entrepreneurs, government officers, police personnel, teachers, lawyers, and engineers. She takes immense pride in having touched their lives and added a little sparkle to their journeys—now, they continue to spread that sparkle wherever they go.

Sanah is a gemologist, crystal healer, numerologist, and Vastu expert. She has touched lives and enriched them.

Beyond her professional life, Sanah finds joy in gardening, meditating, and listening to music. She has a deep appreciation for Chinese cuisine and cherishes moments of peace and reflection.

Motto

My mission is to transform 1 million lives by spreading positive energy into every household through positive parenting. I aspire to create a comprehensive guide for building happy, successful parent-child relationships and fostering harmonious families.

MAY I ASK YOU FOR A SMALL FAVOR?

First, I want to thank you for reading this book. You could have chosen any other book, but you took mine, and I appreciate this. I hope you have at least a few actionable insights that will positively impact your daily life.

Can I ask for 30 seconds more of your time?

I'd love it if you could leave a review of the book. That will help me grow my readership by encouraging folks to take a chance on my books.

Keeping it straight - reviews are the lifeblood of any author.

It will take less than a minute of your time but will tremendously help me reach out to more people.

If you liked this book, please consider posting an honest review on your preferred retailer. And I'd love to see your review. Thanks for your support.